Nelson Grammar

Denis and Helen Ballance

Book 3

Nelson

Contents

Introduction

Grammar is the name given to the rules for writing and speaking English. Because English is spoken in so many parts of the world, it is important that everyone who uses it should keep to the same rules.

Nelson Grammar is a series of books which sets out to explain some of the rules of grammar. The rules given in this book have been chosen because they are the ones you need to know at this stage of your school life. As well as rules dealing with such things as capital letters, punctuation and word order, the books introduce and explain some of the special words used in grammar.

Nelson Grammar is designed to be used alongside your other work in language. Each page spotlights a single grammar topic and is intended to provide the central point for one week's work.

Read the rules and examples given in the blue patches at the top of each page first. After you have studied the rules carefully, do the exercises which provide practice in applying them. Here and there, you will find 'Just for fun' and Revision pages.

At the end of the book, there is an index to help you to look up topics you may need when you are writing. Please do not write the answers to the puzzles and exercises in this book.

Do you remember?

Write these sentences, choosing the correct word from the brackets.

1 Write a (comma   full stop) at the end of the first line of an address.

2 Write a (comma   full stop) after the name of the county in an address.

3 'granite' comes (before   after) 'glove' in a dictionary.

4 He thinks it is (alright   all right) for us to go.

5 They grew (there   their) cucumbers in a frame.

6 A heavy box has (fallen   fell) off the shelf.

7 The plural of 'flash' is ('flashes'   'flashs')

8 'who's' is a short form of ('whose'   'who is')

9 Mary (knowed   knew) them as soon as she saw them.

10 Belfast is a (proper   common) noun.

11 I (won   beat) him at chess.

12 Peter (won   beat) the 50 m race.

13 'camera' has (two   three) syllables.

14 My brothers (works   work) in Leeds.

15 'she' is a (pronoun   adjective).

16 The plural of 'fly' is ('flies'   'flys').

17 Pauline (live   lives) here.

18 (Their   There) is a hair dryer in the cloakroom.

19 Dog is a (proper   common) noun.

20 (Me and Pat   Pat and I) are the fastest runners.

21 ('knives'   'knifes') is the plural of knife.

22 (Mackerels   Mackerel) are caught off Cornwall.

23 'perch' comes (after   between) 'past' and 'poet' in a dictionary.

24 The verb in sentence 11 is in the (past   present) tense.

25 The verb in sentence 10 is in the (past   present) tense.

Do you remember?

A Divide this passage into ten sentences and two paragraphs. Write in capital letters and full stops where they are needed.

all morning greg stalked around the house like a caged tiger breakfast passed him by he could never face food before an important match this was probably the key match of the season a win would place them four points clear of the rest at last the time came to leave for the ground football left his mother cold she could never understand why he was so tense on saturday mornings his father had some inkling of what it was about they both came to the door to see him off

B From the sentences below, pick out and write five verbs, ten plural nouns and ten adjectives.

Mountain sheep roam across the steep hillsides in small groups. The hardy animals are seeking sweet grasses and shrubs. Their dainty feet test the narrow ledges before they go in search of the tempting green shoots. In late spring, the shepherds begin the task of collecting the scattered flocks together.

C Write these sentences. Choose adjectives of your own to fill the spaces.

1 —— seas broke down the —— sea wall.

2 —— walls guarded the —— town.

3 A —— tiger frightened the —— deer.

4 The —— girl rescued two —— children.

D Write these short forms of words and names in full.

Ltd Dept U.S.A. p.t.o. C.I.D. O.H.M.S. Mar. Nov.

Mddx Lieut s.a.e. o.n.o. E.E.C. P.C. Capt. c/o

can't they're doesn't I'm we're didn't couldn't

Sentences, clauses and phrases

A sentence contains a subject and a predicate and is complete in itself.

Example:

I bought some sweets.

You can extend a sentence in two ways.

1 By adding a clause.

Example: I bought some sweets **because I was hungry**.

2 By adding a phrase.

Example: I bought some sweets **in a shop**.

A clause has a subject and a predicate. A phrase has no verb. The original sentence, **I bought some sweets**, becomes a clause of the new, longer sentence.

A Write the numbers of each of these sets of words and say whether the part in blue is a sentence, a clause or a phrase.

1 My Uncle Percy lives alone.   2 His house is off the beaten track.   3 When I go to see him, I catch a bus to Epping.   4 He waits at the bus stop until I arrive.   5 Then we drive out towards North Weald.   6 We have to walk the last two hundred metres because his drive is too rough for cars.   7 I enjoy going to see him although it is a difficult journey.   8 He makes me very welcome

B Write a clause to complete each sentence.

1 We fished all afternoon . . .

2 John went by himself . . .

3 We had to wash all his clothes . . .

4 No-one was seasick . . .

5 The sun shone brightly . . .

6 Jean went home early . . .

Add one word to complete each of these common phrases.

to get your own ——   barking up the wrong ——   on the tip of my ——

to turn a blind ——   as lively as a ——   a storm in a ——

Division of subject and predicate

All sentences divide into at least one subject and one predicate.

Both parts of the sentence may be divided further, like this.

subject		predicate		
extension of subject	subject	verb	extension of verb	completion of verb
My tame	rabbit	nibbled	——	all the corn.
An old	man ·	hobbled	wearily	along the road.

A   Write the subjects and predicates of these sentences in two lists.

1   Our new neighbours have three cats and an Alsatian dog.

2   Heavy lorries grind up the hill all night long.

3   Aston's rubber factory burned for three days and three nights.

4   Joe searched the valley from one end to the other.

5   Silver-barked beeches and stately hornbeams grow on the chalk hills.

B   Make a frame like the one at the top of the page, using the headings in heavy type. Write the parts of these sentences under the correct headings.

1   The old fox sniffed carefully around the trap.

2   We enjoyed our holiday in Torquay very much.

3   John's father ploughed fifteen acres yesterday.

4   A fat man settled himself into one of the chairs.

5   Rich people are not always contented with life.

Change one letter to make each of these words into the name of a metal.   grass   salver   bead   hopper
tip   steed   bold

Commas in lists

Look at this sentence.

Venus, Pluto, Earth and Jupiter are all planets.

The sentence contains a list of four planets.

The last two planet names are joined by **and**. The others are separated by commas.
Venus, Pluto, Earth.

Lists of single words and phrases in sentences are always punctuated in the same way.

A Write the names of the items listed in each of these sentences.

1 The Big Cat House contains lions, tigers, jaguars, leopards and pumas.

2 In July, he visited Douglas, Ramsey, Port Erin, Peel and Castletown.

3 Today's menu includes oxtail soup, roast lamb, chops and plum pie.

B Write these sentences. Put in commas where they are needed.

1 Jim Hugh Alan Tim and Rex are all in the school team this year.

2 The gardens are open on Wednesdays Fridays Saturdays and Sundays.

3 The four ponies' names are Pinto Snow Queen Bay Beauty and Babs.

4 His shop was full of old bottles second-hand furniture cracked china scratched records stuffed birds and general junk.

Write a sentence, containing a list, about each of these pictures.

Commas marking a phrase in apposition

A pair of commas is used to mark off words which are added to a sentence to give extra information.

Example:

Mr Langley, **the next mayor**, was the judge.

the next mayor could be left out.

A phrase like **the next mayor** is said to be in apposition to **Mr Langley**.

A Write the phrases which could be left out of these sentences without changing their meanings.

1 Our new vicar, a native of Blackpool, has three children.

2 The Lewis family, old and young, all went to the seaside.

3 Ann Boleyn, Henry VIII's second wife, died on Tower Green.

B Write these sentences. Put commas round the phrases in apposition.

1 The Bishop of Durham a frail old man preached the sermon.

2 The castle gate grim and forbidding loomed out of the mist.

3 Sir Lancelot brave and true carried the Lion Banner to safety.

4 Mrs Morris Tina's mother has promised to make us some cakes.

5 A dozen bandits followers of Ramon Lopez attacked the mail coach.

Add spaces and punctuation to make these instant sentences. They contain lists and phrases in apposition.

	words	punctuation
1	Theyardwasfullofducksgeeseandturkeys	**,** •
2	Helenmyyoungersisterlikesriding	**, ,** •
3	Ilikecaramelsnougatmintsandrock	**, ,** •
4	Thebucketfulltothebrimfelloffthesteps	**, ,** •

9

Colons

A Write these sentences. Put in colons where they are needed.

1 This is the list of preferred dates May 3rd, June 9th and July 2nd.

2 Here are the ingredients two eggs, butter, flour, parsley and milk.

3 There it was in large letters "Skateboards prohibited on Sundays."

4 These are the chosen players Holden, Moss, Lane, Muir and O'Hare.

5 This is the list of fishing ports Fleetwood, Hull and Grimsby.

B Add spaces and punctuation to make these instant sentences.

	words	punctuation
1	ThesearethewinnersNumbers58and9	: .
2	ThisisthemessageFighttothelastman	: " . "

Copy these word frames on to squared paper. Complete each one with the name of the punctuation mark shown in its circle.

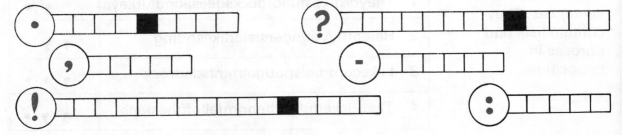

Alphabetical order

To arrange a series of words
which begin with the same two
letters in alphabetical order, use
the third or later letters to decide
the positions.

Examples: archer   armada
arise   armchair
ark   armistice
arrow   armour
artist   army

A Write each of these sets of words in alphabetical order.

1 album	2 liking	3 north	4 cargo	5 water
alert	limit	noun	candy	warm
alcove	lily	nose	cabin	wand
alarm	lion	novel	castle	wall
alder	linnet	notary	cattle	waste

B Make sentences by arranging these jumbled words in alphabetical order.
The first word in each sentence is in blue.

1   even have famous panic generals of moments

2   allied bravely months battled armies to for Zeeland win

3   breathless notes buglers troublesome too find long high

4   a generally June farmer clever harvests in hay

Find a word beginning with bar to fit each picture.
Arrange them in alphabetical order.

1   2   3   4   5   6   7

Revision

A   Divide these simple sentences into subject and predicate.

1 Many wild swans spend the winter in Western Scotland.

2 A mass of swirling, white water poured over the high dam.

3 The racing current hurled the little boat over the waterfall.

B   From the three sentences above, pick out and write three verbs, eight nouns and six adjectives.

C   Write these sentences. Put in commas where they are needed.

1 Matthew Mark Luke and John wrote the four Christian gospels.

2 Mahomet the prophet of Allah was born in Mecca.

3 If you go out after we leave make sure that the door is locked.

4 The sailing dinghy totally helpless was drifting out to sea.

5 Blue skies hot sunshine golden sands and safe bathing are the main ingredients of a good holiday.

D   Write each of these sets of proper nouns in alphabetical order.

1 Burnley, Bolton, Blackpool, Bury, Blackburn, Barrow, Bowness

2 Ayr, Arbroath, Aberdeen, Airdrie, Alloa, Anstruther, Aviemore

3 Merthyr, Swansea, Bridgend, Neath, Treforest, Cardigan, Brecon

4 Coleraine, Belfast, Ballycastle, Portrush, Armagh, Ballymena

E   Write these sentences, putting in colons(:) where they are needed.

1 I heard it on the weather forecast "There will be heavy storms tomorrow."

2 These are the products of Chile copper, citrus fruit and nitrates.

12

Just for fun

A Re-arrange the letters of the words in blue to make the name of each country's capital city.

Italy	China	Greece	Australia	France
more	keg pin	she ant	ban racer	as rip

Nigeria	Holland	New Zealand	Iran	Algeria
goals	mad stream	linnet glow	her tan	leg airs

B Use letters from the words in the middle to make words to fit the pictures.

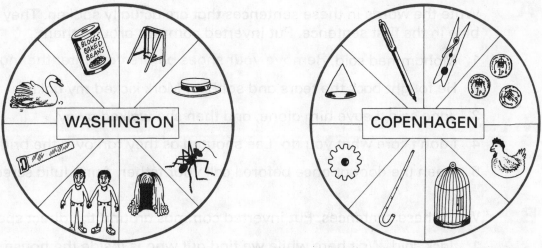

C Remove a letter from each word to make the name of something to wear.

shore carp scandal plants hate stock booty time caper

"OUT OF SIGHT ; OUT OF MIND."

Direct speech

Words actually spoken by a
person are called direct speech.

Direct speech should begin and
end with inverted commas or
speech marks. " . . . "

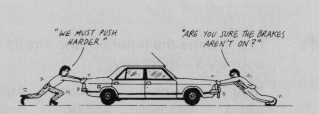

Tom said, "We must push harder."

A Write the words in these sentences that are actually spoken. They are in
blue in the first sentence. Put inverted commas around them.

1   Mohammed said, Remove your shoes before you enter the mosque.

2   He fought back the tears and sobbed, Mark kicked my ankle.

3   Jane said, Leave him alone, and then she walked away.

4   I don't care what you do, Lee shouted as they ran over the bridge.

5   Open the door at once before I call your father, Aunt Julia screamed.

B Write these sentences. Put inverted commas around the direct speech.

1   Jack said, Wait here while we find out who is inside the house.

2   The Captain whispered, Advance to the top of the ridge in open order.

3   Does anyone know who lives in the third house? asked Michelle.

4   You're always the last one to arrive, grumbled Mr Potter.

5   Halt! bellowed the sentry, in a voice that could be heard a mile away.

Write two sentences
in direct speech to
go in the balloons.

Indirect speech

Spoken words that are reported by another person, and not repeated exactly as spoken, are called reported or indirect speech.

Inverted commas are not used for writing indirect speech.

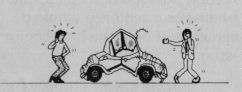

Tom did say that they must push harder.

A   Write the sentences that contain direct speech. Put inverted commas around the words that are actually spoken.

1   Rachel said, I'll meet you outside school at half past four.

2   Martin said that we could leave as soon as we were ready.

3   Miss Grey said, Where did you go for your holiday this year?

4   Paul said that he was late because he had lost his way in the fog.

5   Mr Peters asked us to wait at the entrance to the snack bar.

6   I suppose we shall have to go, said Joseph in a peevish tone.

7   David said, We shall be cut off by the tide if you don't hurry.

8   The Guide Captain announced that the meeting would close early.

Write an account of what happened in the picture-strip below, using only indirect speech.

Punctuation of direct speech

A short passage of direct speech is treated as a sentence within a sentence. It begins with a capital letter.

The direct speech is introduced by words such as **John said, I whispered, We all shouted**, followed by a comma.

Jane said, "I think we ought to wait until Karen arrives."

A   Put in the missing comma and capital letter in each of these sentences. The introductory phrase is in blue.

1   Janet said "where did you put the rest of the chocolates?"

2   Mr Smith said "who was the last person to use the radio?"

3   The sergeant yelled "for goodness sake drop it before it goes off!"

4   Simon muttered "do you think I can afford to wait here all day?"

5   The foreman bawled "right, back to work everybody, at once."

B   Write these sentences. Put in commas, capital letters and inverted commas where they are needed.

1   The policeman said you must always cross at the pelican crossing.

2   Captain Smith ordered stand by to abandon ship at short notice.

3   Somebody in the crowd shouted whose side is the referee on?

4   The unhappy man stammered all I want is to be left in peace.

Write a sentence about this picture including the direct speech that might be in the balloon.

Divided direct speech

Words such as **John said, I whispered**, that introduce direct speech may come before, in the middle of or at the end of the words actually spoken.

Examples:

Ann said, "What are we waiting for?"

"What," **said Ann**, "are we waiting for?"

"What are we waiting for?" **said Ann**.

A   Write the words in these sentences that are actually spoken.

    1   The steward said, Do you take tea or coffee, sir?

    2   If pressed to make a choice, replied Mr Briggs, I prefer tea.

    3   I regret, sir, that there is only coffee, answered the steward.

B   Write sentences 1, 2 and 3 again, adding inverted commas.

C   Write these sentences, putting in all necessary punctuation.

    1   I have been chosen to be the Rose Queen boasted Samantha.

    2   And whose mother sneered Gillian is the head of the committee?

    3   Samantha pouted and said That's got nothing at all to do with it.

Write each of the short passages of direct speech from the black box. Add the best ending from the blue box to complete each sentence.

"I don't think that's fair,"	shrieked Ben.
"There's a skeleton in there,"	ordered Jack.
"I'm certain that it is true,"	grumbled Brian.
"That's a very funny story,"	insisted Monica.
"Stay exactly where you are,"	chuckled Rex.

Divided direct speech

Look at these two sentences.

1   "It is a goal," he said, "because the ball is in the net."

2   "It is a goal," he said. "The ball is in the net."

In 1, the direct speech is all one sentence, but it has been divided. The second part of it begins with a small letter.
There are two sentences in 2. The second one begins with a capital.

A   Say whether there are one or two sentences in the direct speech in each of the following.

1   While the money lasted he said it was a most enjoyable life.

2   Today we have ten men he said tomorrow there will be thirty.

B   There are two sentences of direct speech in each of the following. Add commas, inverted commas and full stops.

1   My brother is a sailor I said He will be home at the end of May

2   This is my final offer he said You can take it or leave it

3   His aunt is a very old lady Judith said She lives in Taunton

C   Add capital letters and all necessary punctuation to these sentences.

1   please give me a hand said john this box is very heavy

2   while I am alive said uncle tom no-one cuts down that tree

Fill in the missing letters to make words that can introduce direct speech.

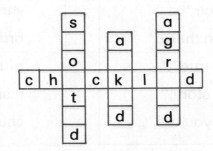

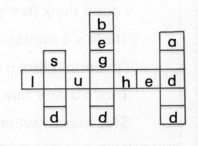

Direct speech in stories

Most writers use direct speech to tell their stories. It makes the characters appear more life-like.

When writing a conversation, it is usual to begin the words of each new speaker about 20 mm in from the left-hand margin.

A Read this conversation.

"What's all this about giants?" Hans asked as soon as they were alone.

"I don't know, but everybody seems very frightened," said Karl, "particularly the Baron. Fancy offering half his lands as a reward!"

"Just think of what you could do with the reward," he went on, after a moment's thought. "I've a good mind to try my luck."

Hans stared at him in amazement.

"You!" he burst out. "How could you take on two giants? You wouldn't dare."

Karl, who was much shorter than his friend, looked at Hans mischievously.

"Oh I don't know," he said. "I don't suppose the giants are very clever. Big people rarely are."

B Answer these questions in sentences.

1 How many people took part in the conversation?

2 Who had offered a reward?

3 Which of the two friends was keen to win the reward?

4 Write three words with the same meaning as said that are used in the conversation.

5 Write all the short forms of words you can find.

Continue the conversation in your own words.
Make Karl persuade his friend to join him in trying to win the reward.

Making opposites: in and im

The opposites of some words may be formed by writing **in** or **im** in front of them.

Examples:

secure→ insecure
proper→ improper

A Write in in front of these words to make their opposites.

formal definite competent elegant offensive attentive

B Write im in front of these words to make their opposites.

mature perfect practical permanent mortal possible pure

C Write these sentences. Form opposites from the words in blue to fill the spaces.

The volcano was thought to be —— and ——
of erupting again. On that May morning, the
villagers heard —— rumbles from deep
underground. A few —— people started to
climb the cone to see what was happening.
Then, without warning, the —— eruption happened.

in

distinct famous

active capable

cautious

It was —— to get through to the village. The
road was blocked by —— drifts of cinder and
proved ——. —— as the rescue teams were
to get in to the area, they found themselves ——.

im

passable mobile

movable patient

possible

Choose one of the words in blue to fit each of these meanings.

1 not fit to eat

2 lacking some parts

3 not lasting

4 not to be seen

5 mad

6 cheap

incomplete invisible
impermanent inexpensive
inedible insane

Gender

Some nouns have masculine and feminine forms. This difference in form is called gender.

Examples:

prince   princess

Nouns which include both masculine and feminine have common gender.

Examples:

doctor   patient

Nouns which are names of things neither masculine nor feminine are called neuter.

Examples:

stool   jug

A   Write these sentences. Change all the masculines, in blue, into feminines.

1   His brother asked the policeman to show him where the mayor lived.

2   The boy saw the fox seize the gander and run into the wood.

3   We heard that the waiter was the heir to the estate of Lord Lee.

B   Write these nouns in four lists under the headings MASCULINE, FEMININE, COMMON and NEUTER.

drake   cousin   widow   deer   tree   cardinal   maiden   tank   uncle

filly   valley   boar   visitor   wire   squaw   librarian   prisoner

Copy this puzzle on squared paper. Fill in the answers. The blue panel will spell out a neuter noun.

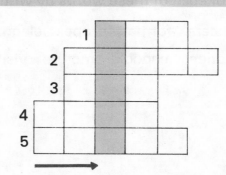

1   feminine of boar

2   masculine of actress

3   feminine of buck

4   feminine of uncle

5   feminine of king

Revision

A Write these sentences. In place of each ⁎, put in speech marks and other missing punctuation.

1 Llewellyn said ⁎ ⁎If you wait until this afternoon ⁎ I will go with you ⁎

2 ⁎The most powerful of all the gods ⁎ declared Mr Timms ⁎ ⁎was Thor ⁎

3 ⁎Don⁎t you ever stop eating ⁎ exclaimed Miss Greenwood indignantly ⁎

B Punctuate this passage.

As soon as the Baron was sure that the Giant had gone he said
Why did you open the gates Someone will go to the dungeon for
this outrage Where were the guards
The steward dropped to his knees and wrung his hands
What could I do master he whined The Giant was breaking down the
doors You cannot have forgotten what Albrecht did in your father's time
The whole country side was laid waste
At the mention of Albrecht's name the Baron blanched and sat down
What are we to do he whimpered The Giants will ruin me

C Write these nouns in four lists under the headings MASCULINE, FEMININE, COMMON and NEUTER.

friend stone heifer mountain father heroine relation nephew
baron river elephant vixen sister castle citizen cock jug
countess boar knife pony husband ewe parent

D Make the opposite of each of these words by writing in or im in front of it.

possible pure sincere formal proper elegant sane perfect
human secure patient capable mature visible tolerable

Just for fun

A Each of these shapes contains the name of an occupation. Re-arrange the letters to find each one.

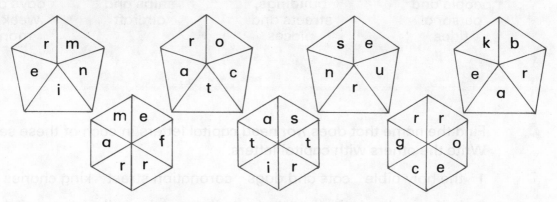

B This message is not what it appears to be. Read every fourth word, starting with the first, to find out what the real message is.

The chief insists on new arrangements for contacting Captain Smith. Walk out of Ashley to the Police Box and you will, just before noon, be able to see waiting, a hand cart for collecting litter. When you reach it, stand by the cart until the watchman opens the bridge. If you are late, do not use this method. In the afternoon, he lies low.

C Change one letter in each of these words to make the name of a fruit.

apply pig grave grange dare perch

cheery time demon tango hear slum

"LOOK BEFORE YOU LEAP."

When to use capital letters

Use capitals to begin sentences and for these names:

Mr Smith	**Oak Street**	**Trident**	**Monday**
people and personal titles	buildings, streets and places	ships and aircraft	days of the week and months

A Find the name that does *not* need capital letters in each of these sets. Write the others with capital letters.

1 the holy bible   cats and dogs   coronation street   king charles

2 balfour school   ford granada   railway arch   kellogg's cornflakes

3 low tide   royal artillery   wimbledon football club   saint peter

4 christmas eve   dr anna dobson   westminster abbey   seven o'clock

5 british petroleum   thomas nelson   poppy seed   easter sunday

6 h.m.s. hermes   the royal mint   pop music   cumberland avenue

7 the koran   the boy scouts   vegetable marrow   northern ireland

8 dorset road   north america   robinson crusoe   herring gull

B Write a sentence for each box, containing all the words in it.

Sandra   London
February   I

Italian   June
Bond Street

Think of capital letters which, if written in front of these sets of letters, will make them into proper nouns. Work across both pages.

Example:

M { onday / artha / alaya   { oland / amela / inner   { obin / ussia / amsey   { xford / swald / liver   { lymouth / atricia / ortugal   { aster / urope / xeter

Jesus	**Robin Hood**	**B.B.C.**	**Airfix**	**African**
sacred names	books, films and plays	'I' by itself and initials	companies, products and clubs	adjectives made from names

A Write this passage. Put in capital letters where they are needed.

mrs peake and her daughter, lana lechlade, left for america on new year's day. they travelled from bolton to london airport and stayed overnight at the skyway hotel. on friday morning, they took off in a british airways boeing jumbo jet for new york.

they will stay in that city until january 10th with mrs peake's sister, caroline. later, they will fly on to ohio to visit mrs lechlade's son, tom, who works for the u. s. government. they will reach los angeles early in february. while they are away, i am looking after samson and sheba, their two boxer dogs.

B This is an illuminated capital letter. The monks who used to copy out hand-written books drew them as decorations. Could you draw one? Try one or both of your initials.

When you have found the answers, write the capital letters in the order given to make two words. The words tell you what part of speech your answers are.

{ oberts
{ omford
{ umania

{ ovember
{ uneaton
{ ebraska

{ ctober
{ rkneys
{ ntario

{ ranus
{ rsula
{ ganda

{ igeria
{ orfolk
{ eptune

{ cotland
{ aturday
{ amantha

25

Comparison of adjectives

Compare the heights of the three things in the picture.

1 John is **tall**.

2 The bus is **taller** than John.

3 The tower is the **tallest** of the three.

Adjectives have three steps or degrees of comparison. They are

1 positive   **tall**

2 comparative   **taller**

3 superlative   **tallest**

A   Add er to these positive forms of adjectives to make them comparative.

high   deep   few   slow   cold   strong   hard   rough   steep   loud   long

old   fresh   damp   clean   straight   mild   thick   soft   smooth   short

B   Add est to these positives to change them into superlatives.

bold   dull   stiff   dark   fair   clear   fast   sharp   swift   weak   new

bright   warm   wild   low   plain   light   tough   small   great   broad

C   Write these sentences. Change the adjectives, in blue, into comparatives.

1   Gold is dear than silver.

2   Summer is hot than winter.

3   Christopher is the fast runner.

4   Jane is quick at passing the ball.

Write the names of the things in each circle in order of their real size, starting with the smallest.

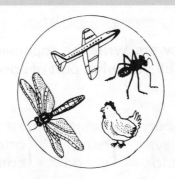

Adjectives: comparative

The comparative degree, ending in **er**, is used to compare two things.

Example:

He is older than me.

The comparative of a long adjective is formed by writing **more** in front of it.

The comparative of an adjective ending in **y** is made by changing **y** to **ier**.

A Write these sentences. Change the long adjectives, in blue, into comparatives.

1 The snake is frightened than he is.
2 Her friendship is precious than gold.
3 Try to be careful next time.
4 This guest is even important

B Write the comparative forms of these adjectives.

lively merry heavy sleepy pretty happy mighty dusty

noisy sunny dainty flimsy tidy jolly busy wealthy

C Write these sentences. Change the adjectives, in blue, into comparatives.

1 This engine is the noisy of the two.
2 The lake is deep than the pool.
3 Do try to be friendly towards him.
4 Her voice is high than mine.
5 My pony is the frisky of the two.
6 Antrim is beautiful than ever.

Long adjectives are usually considered to be those with more than one syllable, although those ending in y are exceptions.

Write the nine long adjectives in this list.

blazing new reliable important brave

ladylike fit leisurely broad immense

late ancient tame nervous thoughtful

Write the first letters of the nine you have chosen in the order in which they appear in the list. If they are correct, they will spell a word meaning very bright

Adjectives: superlative

The superlative degree, ending in **est**, is used to compare three or more things.	The superlative of a long adjective is made by writing **most** in front of it.	The superlative of an adjective ending in **y** is made by changing **y** to **iest**.
Example:	**Example:**	**Example:**
He is the **oldest** player	**most** attractive	lovely → loveliest

A   Write the superlative degree of these adjectives.

light   jolly   late   pleasant   near   intelligent   popular   safe
awkward   nasty   important   fine   savage   comfortable   profitable

B   Write these sentences. Change the adjectives, in blue, to the correct degree.

1   He is the tall of the guardsmen.   3   Jack is the brave of the three.

2   Cycling is quick than walking.   4   Carol is the young of all.

C   Complete these tables of degrees of comparison.

positive	comparative	superlative
fast	faster	fastest
fair	——	——
sunny	——	——
tight	——	——

positive	comparative	superlative
modern	more modern	most modern
terrible	——	——
sincere	——	——
violent	——	——

Find an adjective, beginning with the letters shown, to describe each line.

cu   ho   ve   di   do

Comparison of irregular adjectives

Learn these irregular forms.

positive	comparative	superlative	positive	comparative	superlative
good	better	best	shy	shyer	shyest
bad	worse	worst	sly	slyer	slyest
little	less	least	fit fat		
			hot wet	double the last	
			thin sad	consonant	
some			grim dim		
many	more	most			
much			e.g. big	bigger	biggest

A   Write these sentences, choosing the correct word from the brackets.

1   Peter's dog is the (bigger   biggest) one in the whole show.

2   The teacher said that my work was (worse   worst) than yours.

3   Of all the girls, Marian has done (more   most) to help the team.

B   Write these sentences. Change the adjectives, in blue, to the correct degree.

1   I have done little than Jean but Lynne has done the little of all.

2   She gained the high marks because she is the good jumper here.

3   Brazil is big, hot and wet than Mexico.

4   I don't know whether it is bad to be the thin or the fat in the class.

Write an adjective to compare the blue figure in each circle with the black ones.

Adjectives: no comparison

Some adjectives have no degrees of comparison.

For example, we cannot say **more unique** or **most unique** because unique means one of a kind and so cannot be compared.

It is the same with number adjectives and adjectives indicating time.

Examples:

twenty   daily

A   Write the adjectives in these lists that can exist only in the positive.

1   three   light   next   triangular   fierce   both   steady   weekly   no

2   first   left   happy   important   several   square   evergreen   monthly

3   wooden   one   new   right   daily   dim   gold   all   main   enough

Take the first letters of the adjectives you have written from List 3. Put them together to spell out two words describing what you have just been doing.

B   Write these sentences. Replace the adjectives in blue with their comparatives or superlatives.

It was the cold morning of the year, but Scott retained his record as the early riser. Oates's frostbite was bad than ever. Food was scarce and their rations were small than Scott considered desirable. That morning, the snow was deep than ever and the bad blizzard they had yet encountered kept them inside the tent all day.

Write a sentence containing a comparative or superlative adjective for each balloon.

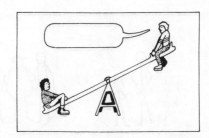

30

Using indefinite articles

a and **an** are indefinite articles. Write **a** before a word starting with a consonant. Write **an** before a word starting with a vowel.

There are two exceptions.

1 Write **an** before a silent **h**.

2 Write **a** before **u** and **eu** when they sound like **y**.

A   Make a list, in alphabetical order, of the words beginning with vowels.

familiar asteroid entrance interior yearling urchin optician uncle director racket order argument insect certainty exit

B   Write these sentences. Fill each space with either a or an.

1 We saw — fine example of — Eurovision programme last night.

2 Dr Smith received — honorary degree from — university in America.

3 There is nothing like — eucalyptus tree to remind — Australian of home.

4 The car plant produced rather more than — unit — hour in 1978.

5 — electric car would be — useful vehicle if you lived in — urban district.

Change the y into another letter in each of the words in the box to make
1 the names of 10 living creatures. 2 four words to fit the pictures.

story	pray	may	any
yell	yard	myth	
sway	year	yule	guy
stay	pulley	bay	

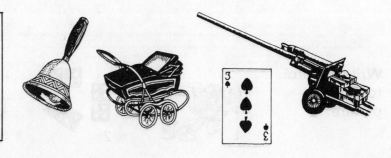

Plurals: words ending in o

Musical terms and names of musical instruments ending in **o** add **s** to form their plurals.

Example:

soprano → sopranos

Most other words ending in **o** add **es** to make their plurals.

Example:

potato → potatoes

Words ending in **oo** always form their plurals by adding **s**.

Example:

cuckoo → cuckoos

Learn these exceptions:

Eskimos or Eskimoes

lidos   curios   photos

solos   radios   kimonos

hippos   memos   folios

rhinos   lassos

A   Write these sentences. Change the words ending in o into their plurals. Make the verbs in blue agree with their subjects in number.

1. The last echo of the cello was drowned by the entry of the piano.

2. Fields of tomato and potato grew in the shadow of the volcano.

3. The photo showed that the cargo was not as listed in the memo.

4. All the soprano and contralto were given kimono as memento.

5. The Eskimo who visited the zoo stared at the hippo and cockatoo in amazement.

B   Write the plurals of these words.

hero   negro   halo   solo   alto   cello   piccolo   lido   curio   folio

Write a plural to fit each picture.

1

2

3

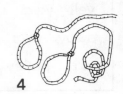
4

Plurals: compound words

Most compound words contain a main word.

This main word, usually the second, should be made plural.

Examples: golf-clubs   bedrooms

Notice: brothers-in-law, fathers-in-law, sisters-in-law, coats-of-arms, lookers-on, passers-by, menservants.

A Write these sentences. Change all the words in blue into plurals.

1 He was giving handful of leaflets to all the passer-by.

2 Mr Lynd always visits his two brother-in-law at weekend.

3 The man on the ledge threw bucketful of water over the looker-on.

4 Painted on the sides of the tank-transporter were their regimental coat-of-arms.

5 The bye-law include strict rules about trading in the market-place.

B Write the plurals of these words.

mine-sweeper   mouse-trap   safety-pin   war-cry   spoonful

major-general   by-way   mother-in-law   burglar-alarm

son-in-law   fare-stage   dog-biscuit   coachman   alarm-clock

Write the plurals of the compound names suggested by these pictures.

1   2   3   4   5

Revision

A   Write this passage. Put in capital letters where they are needed.

anna yeung ho comes from hong kong. she came to live in britain at the end of last february. her parents run the golden lion chinese restaurant in bristol. at first, she knew only a few words of english but, at railton street primary school, she has made many friends and her progress in learning the language has been excellent. she now helps her mother to read the television times and they both enjoy watching blue peter and nationwide.

B   Write the plurals of these words.

tomato   hero   mother-in-law   cello   halo   guard-of-honour   trio

piano   kangaroo   by-stander   radio   volcano   tank-transporter

C   Write these sentences. Change the adjectives, in blue, to the correct degree of comparison.

1 Your bike is good than Elizabeth's.

2 The book is even silly than I thought.

3 Carol is the tall girl in the group.   7 Truth is strange than fiction.

4 Don is the reliable patrol-leader.   8 Mars is near than Jupiter.

5 My dog is intelligent than yours.   9 His is the bad of them all.

6 Paul Peters is heavy than you.   10 This is the good story in the set.

D   Write these phrases with either a or an in front of them.

unusual noise   European city   honest man   useful book

hour's break   unlucky number   yellow car   late arrival

used car   honourable settlement   pale colour   united front

Just for fun

A Complete these word chains. One letter must be changed at each stage and each step must be a real word.

Example: (answers in blue)   word   ward   wand   wane   wage   page

tall —— tilt —— tiny   cone —— cord ford —— wood

chop —— stop —— stew   hard —— cart cast —— easy

book —— cork —— worm   lane —— lend lead —— road

B Take letters from the end of the first word and the beginning of the second to make collective nouns. The word in blue gives a clue.

Example: soldiers   warm yellow → w(arm y)ellow → army

lions   troop rider   cows   feather duster   trees   before standing

dogs   split territory   horses   best ringer   robbers   raging anger

sailors   public reward   footballers   late ambulance

rioters   random observer   loaves   combat challenge

C Find the names of seven fruits in this square. You may move from one letter to the next in any direction.

a	p	u	m	o
r	p	l	e	n
i	e	r	r	y
c	h	e	a	h
o	t	p	a	c

Proverbial Fun

"AN APPLE A DAY KEEPS THE DOCTOR AWAY."

Prepositions

A preposition is a word that shows the relationship between two nouns or pronouns.

Examples:

The car is **near** our gate.

We waited **with** Katherine.

The lamb is **in** the field.

Our plane is **over** London.

A   Write these sentences. Choose the best preposition in blue to fill each space.

between   under   near   through   at   into   round   for   off   on

1   The car sped —— the corner and ran —— a double-decker bus.

2   Simon banged his head —— the ceiling and fell —— the steps.

3   Their house is —— the bridge half way —— Rhos and Flint.

4   We shouted —— help as the boat sank —— the waves.

5   The leading car crashed —— the barrier —— reckless speed.

B   Find seven pairs of opposites in this list of prepositions.

inside	before	without	off
from	up	to	down	under	on
outside	with	over	after

Write sentences about the picture containing the prepositions in the box.

behind	opposite	near
between	above	below

Prepositions linked with particular words

Certain prepositions are usually linked with particular words.

Example:

Paula **suffers from** headaches.

Learn: ashamed **of**   similar **to**   filled **with**
full **of**   good **for**   angry **with**   guilty **of**
protest **against**   rely **on**   disappointed **with**

Notice: I agree **with** you.   I agreed **to** stay.
He parted **with** his car.   I parted **from** them.

A   Write these sentences. Choose the correct preposition to fill each space.

1   The shop was full —— people.

2   Do not rely —— me to attend.

3   Helen always agrees —— Janet.

4   The captain is disappointed —— me.

5   Nick is suffering —— the 'flu.

6   He was found guilty —— burglary.

7   The dress is similar —— mine.

8   My Easter egg is filled —— sweets.

B   Find ten prepositions in these sentences.

Mountain gorillas are found in Central Africa. They live in troops amongst high mountain ranges. They wander through the forest looking for fruit and roots. Movement depends upon the weather, but they usually cover between two and three miles each day. Gorillas live on the ground, although younger ones will climb trees after fruit, sometimes throwing some of it down to the older members of the tribe.

Find the prepositions hidden in these words. **Example:** supply → s(up)ply → up

foundered   leather   pyramids   training   toffee   hovering   information

Three common mistakes

teach and **learn**

If the person who does the teaching is the subject of the sentence, use the verb **to teach**.
If the subject is the learner, use the verb **to learn**.

bought and **brought**

bought is the past tense of the verb **to buy**.
brought is the past tense of the verb **to bring**.

between and **among**

Use the preposition **between** if only two people or things are involved.
If there are more than two, use **among**.

A   Write these sentences. Fill the spaces with one or other of the words in the boxes opposite each set of sentences.

| teach |
| learn |

1   You must —— to swim before you are allowed in a canoe.

2   Mr Hughes and Miss Lee —— us to swim at the Baths.

3   If you ask them, they will —— you in the evenings.

| bought |
| brought |

4   John Smith —— a stuffed crocodile to school yesterday.

5   His father —— it in an antique shop in Edinburgh.

6   A big game hunter —— it back from East Africa in 1925.

| between |
| among |

7   We had only thirty pence —— the five of us.

8   Linda and I bought a bar of chocolate —— us.

Match a word from the blue box with each number in the black box.

| one two three four eight |
| ten twelve twenty hundred |
| one hundred and forty-four |

| century gross trio decade |
| octet score unit quartet |
| dozen brace |

Verbs: the infinitive

The infinitive is the part of the verb which can always have **to** written in front of it. When we refer to verbs we always use the present infinitive.

Examples:

to drink   to remember

The auxiliary verbs **can, could, would, must, will, shall, should, might** and **may** are followed by the infinitive.

Examples:

can go   might want

Avoid splitting an infinitive by writing another word between **to** and the rest of the verb.

A   Write these sentences. Choose an infinitive from below to fill each space.

swim   give   swallow   join   return   write

1   She will —— this afternoon.

2   Tom can —— under water.

3   We could —— a letter.

4   You must —— the pill.

5   You should —— the Guides.

6   I shall —— him a pound.

B   Pick out and write the infinitive from each of these sentences.

1   He tried to forget them.

2   I used to sing in the choir.

3   You could break a window.

4   You must arrive early.

5   They might come tomorrow.

6   Rabbits like to burrow.

C   One sentence in each of these pairs contains a split infinitive. The other is correct. Write the correct sentence from each pair.

1   We hope to shortly visit India.
    We hope to visit India shortly.

2   They tried to not get involved.
    They tried not to get involved.

Find the infinitives in this letter line. They all begin with blue letters.

S I N G R O W E A V E N G E T A M E E T R U S T R E T C H A S E T

Subject and verb agreement

Verbs and their subjects must agree in number.

Examples:

John stops. (singular)

Buses stop. (plural)

Each and **every** always introduce singular subjects.

Example:

Every policeman **wears** a helmet.

Collective nouns are always singular.

Example:

The committee sits tomorrow.

A Write these sentences, choosing the correct form of the verb from the brackets.

1 Uncle John (like   likes) peanuts.

2 The chairs (need   needs) cushions.

3 The twins (wear   wears) jeans.

4 Every bunch of grapes (grows   grow) on the old shoots.

5 A bunch of keys (is   are) missing.

6 Lord Bullen's tenants (refuses   refuse) to pay their rents.

7 The Atlantic Fleet (was   were) lying at Invergordon.

8 A long column of soldiers (advance   advances) across the plain.

B Write the ten subjects from this list that are followed by singular verbs.

choir   postmen   regiment   oxen   crowd   tribe   cattle   herd

a pair of trousers   mice   pack   two   boats   flock   crew   team

Write the collective noun for a group of:

1   2   3   4   5   6   7

Auxiliary verbs with special uses

can and **may**

can means **is able to.**

Example: He **can** remember.

may means **has permission to.**

Example: You **may** begin.

shall and **will**

Write **shall** after I and we.
Write **will** after you, they, he, she and it.
To make a strong statement, write them the other way round.

Example: (ordinary statement)
I **shall** wait here until he comes.

Example: (strong statement)
You **shall** do your homework!

A Write these sentences. Write may or can in each space.

1 Jo —— speak French fluently.

2 —— John come out now?

3 The puppy —— sit up and beg.

4 You —— take it for a walk.

5 From here, you —— see the sea.

6 You —— go down to the beach.

B These sentences make ordinary statements. Write them putting shall or will in each space.

1 I —— be waiting at the station.

2 They —— not be expecting us.

3 The car —— be there at eleven.

4 We —— watch from a window.

5 The race —— start from York.

6 Any date —— suit Anthea.

Choose the sentence that matches each picture.

You shall go to bed.
You will go to bed.

You shall drive slowly.
You will drive slowly.

I shall see the match.
I will see the match.

Adverbs

Adverbs tell us how, when cr where the action of a verb takes place.

Example:
Snails crawl.
Snails crawl **slowly**.

The adverb **slowly** tells us how snails crawl.

Many adverbs end in **ly**, but all words ending in **ly** are not adverbs.

A   Look at these sentences. For each one, write a) the verb and b) the adverb that tells you how, when or where the action of the verb takes place.

1   Paul chewed the sweet slowly.
2   He climbed painfully to the top.
3   The otter slipped away at once.
4   We paddled after them furiously.
5   All summer, Granma lived alone.
6   He often visited their homes.
7   It rained hard all morning.
8   She always comes on Fridays.

B   Write these sentences. Fill in the spaces with suitable adverbs from the list in blue.

slowly   intensely   angrily   desperately   twice   never

1   I walked ——, trying —— to avoid catching the bull's attention.
2   The tiger —— drank at the same spot ——.
3   They disliked each other —— and never met without quarrelling ——

Write eight different adverbs of your own to tell how the actions of these verbs took place.

The dog ate ——.
The dog barked ——.
The dog snarled ——.
The dog ran ——.

The dog chased the stick ——.
The dog hid the bone ——.
The dog wagged its tail ——.
The dog howled ——.

Comparison of adverbs

Adverbs have degrees of comparison. They are formed in the same ways as degrees of comparison of adjectives.

positive	comparative	superlative
slowly	more slowly	most slowly
fast	faster	fastest

Some adverbs tell us more about other adverbs.

Examples:

so very rather more most even less only

He fell **rather** heavily.

Please walk **less** quickly.

A Write these sentences. Make the adverbs, in blue, into comparatives.

1 Everyone scrambled to safety as the boat began to sink quickly.

2 The men in the trenches fought bravely after the shelling stopped.

3 When we move to Bristol, we shall be able to visit you often.

4 After the petrol tank exploded, the fire began to burn fiercely.

B Write the two adverbs in each sentence that tell you more about the verb in blue.

1 I was waiting very patiently.

2 The bus is running rather late.

3 Defeat makes him try even harder.

4 Do try to shoot more carefully.

5 Don't talk so loudly.

6 Peter works quite hard.

Take letters from the end of the first word and the beginning of the second to make adverbs.

Example: tinsel dome → tin(sel dom)e → seldom

sofa stuffing   unsafe lying   one verse   soft entrance   vehicles stop

Similes and metaphors

Similes and metaphors paint word pictures that make speech more vivid and descriptions more colourful.

A simile: One thing is compared with another, often using the word **like**.

Example:

Her hair is like copper.

A metaphor: Words, not normally put together, are used to give a striking impression.

Example:

a jungle of alleys

A   Write the word pictures in these sentences. Say whether they are similes or metaphors.

1   Her hair was as white as snow.

2   Tarzan has an iron grip.

3   Damp trees supported the heavy sky.

4   The night was as black as pitch.

5   The church is as old as the hills.

6   Angry waves clawed at the boat.

7   His face would turn the milk sour.

8   He roared like a lion.

B   Complete these sentences with your own word pictures.

The mist lay over the moor like . . . . My hands and feet were as cold as . . . . Dark trees loomed out of the mist like . . . . Not a sound broke the . . . . My spine tingled with . . . . All at once, an owl swept by. It hooted twice, like a . . . . and I heard the . . . . of panic-stricken mice in the dry leaves under the hedge.

Animal names are often used in word pictures. Which of the animals named in the blue box is supposed to possess the qualities shown in the black box?

| elephant   fox   bear |
| mule   owl   lion |

| bad temper   good memory   bravery |
| stubbornness   wisdom   cunning |

Letter writing: opening and closing

Open all letters with **Dear . . . ,** When you write a business letter, put the name and address of the company at X.

If you are writing to someone you know, close the letter with **Yours sincerely** at Y. If the letter is to someone whose name you do not know, end it with **Yours faithfully**.

Read this business letter.

```
                                              ┌─────────────┐
                                              │      A       │
                                              ├─────────────┤
                                              │      B       │
                                              └─────────────┘
The P.R.S. Mail Order Co.
Lazonbridge,
Wiltshire.


Dear Sirs,

     On February 15th I ordered a model aircraft kit from
you. The kit was for a Douglas D.C. 10. I enclosed a postal
order for £1-65 to cover the cost of the kit and postage. The
kit arrived yesterday but, when I opened it, I discovered that
it is a kit for a Hawker Hurricane and that some of the parts
are missing. Before I return it, I should like to know whether
you are willing to pay the postage. This amounts to 33p. I
suggest that you send me the correct, complete kit and enclose
the return postage for the Hurricane kit.

                              ┌─────────────┐
                              │      C       │
                              └─────────────┘
                              Alan Glover
```

Write the letter again. Write your own address at A, today's date at B and the correct ending at C. Divide the letter into three paragraphs.

Revision

A Write these sentences, choosing the correct word from the brackets.

1 Miss Hampson is(learning teaching) me to play the piano.

2 Neither Jill nor Wendy(like likes) to be left out.

3 Ask your mother whether you(may can) go with us to London.

4 I(shall will) be surprised if his opinion differs(from to) mine.

5 Jock and I had agreed to share the reward(between among) us.

6 Lynn's father(bought brought) us home from school in his car.

7 Everybody(are is) expected to be back by half past eleven.

B Find five nouns, five adjectives, five verbs, five adverbs and five prepositions in this passage. Write them in lists.

    Nature has cleverly devised the leaf fall to protect trees against the harsh winter weather. As the days grow colder, a hard skin forms between the leaf and the twig, quickly cutting off the supply of sap.

    The tree is battening down for the winter, deliberately leaving the tender leaves to shrivel and die. Soon they will fall to the ground beneath the tree and eventually return to the soil.

C Some similes are over-used. Choose new words to replace those in blue.

1 as cold as ice

2 as heavy as lead

3 as brave as a lion

4 as light as a feather

5 as quiet as a mouse

6 as white as snow

D Copy and complete this table of degrees of comparison of adverbs.

positive	comparative	superlative
sadly	——	——
——	more deeply	——
——	more strongly	——
——	——	most vividly

Just for fun

A Change one letter in each word to make the name of a number.

fight   fine   ore   throe   sever   give   tan   hour   fix

B Re-arrange the letters of the words in the middle of the circle to make anagrams to fit the numbered spaces.

The last letter of each anagram is also the first letter of the next. Number One is already filled in.

11

1 s m i l e

10

9

8

7 6 5 4 3 2

1 miles
2 den   3 reed
4 bury   5 pay
6 tap   7 meat
8 live   9 owl
10 flow
11 fist

C Change the first letter of each of these words to make the name of a bird.

cove   full   park   brow   hook   boot   loose   sit   luck
clover   bay   haven

Proverbial Fun

PLEASE GO AWAY!

"HE WHO PAYS THE PIPER, CALLS THE TUNE."

Index